LOVE POEMS

Biblioasis International Translation Series
General Editor: Stephen Henighan

I Wrote Stone: The Selected Poetry of Ryszard Kapuściński (Poland)
    Translated by Diana Kuprel and Marek Kusiba

Good Morning Comrades by Ondjaki (Angola)
    Translated by Stephen Henighan

Kahn & Engelmann by Hans Eichner (Austria-Canada)
    Translated by Jean M. Snook

Dance With Snakes by Horacio Castellanos Moya (El Salvador)
    Translated by Lee Paula Springer

Black Alley by Mauricio Segura (Quebec)
    Translated by Dawn M. Cornelio

The Accident by Mihail Sebastian (Romania)
    Translated by Stephen Henighan

Love Poems by Jaime Sabines (Mexico)
    Translated by Colin Carberry

LOVE POEMS

Jaime Sabines

Translated from the Spanish by Colin Carberry

BIBLIOASIS

First published as *Poesía amorosa. Selección y prólogo de Mario Benedetti* by Seix Barral, Mexico City, 1988.

FIRST EDITION

Library and Archives Canada Cataloguing in Publication

Sabines, Jaime
    Love poems / Jaime Sabines ; translated from the Spanish by Colin Carberry.

ISBN 978-1-926845-30-2

    I. Carberry, Colin, 1972- II. Title.

PQ7297.S2A2 2011   861'.64   C2011-903437-9

Edited by Stephen Henighan

PRINTED AND BOUND IN CANADA

para Verónica y Kathleen, mis bien amadas

CONTENTS

INTRODUCTION

I had been living in Linares, a small, northern Mexican city, for about six months before I heard of Jaime Sabines. A year earlier I had backpacked through El Salvador, Guatemala, and Mexico, visiting everything I found of interest from La Libertad to the Texas border, before dwindling funds cut short my three-month adventure. Back in Toronto, I pined for Mexico, and for the remainder of that long, gruelling winter diligently studied the country's history and literature in preparation for my return. But during my first lonely months in Linares I was haunted by the notion that something fundamental was eluding me.

Then it happened. Ostensibly to improve my limited Spanish, I had begun to meet for coffee with a charming young teacher from Colegio Linares, the private school where we both worked. When Verónica read me the opening lines of a prose poem in the Hotel Plaza (my habitual writing place) one rainy August afternoon I felt a sharp, intensely pleasing, visceral shock.

> I HOPE TO BE CURED OF YOU one of these days. I have to stop smoking you, drinking you, thinking you. It's possible, following the moral guidelines of our times. I prescribe time, abstinence, solitude.

It dawned on me that I had stumbled upon a major poet. So why hadn't I heard of this Jaime Sabines?

Some time after attending a cultural event at the local theatre which featured an effusive recitation of another of Sabines's prose poems, "I Love You at Ten in the Morning," one of us turned on the car radio to hear the same poem fading through the poorly tuned static... On November 2nd, the Day of the Dead, stopping to admire the *altares de muertos* that my pupils had erected in memory of famous Mexicans, I spotted a framed photograph of a mustachioed, curly-haired man with thick glasses and vaguely Arabic features grinning mischievously from behind a haze of cigarette smoke. I must have commented on this, because the following morning a student loaned me her mother's copy of a selection of Sabines's work. The author photo on the cover was the same one I had seen atop the *altar*. Two days later, the school principal handed me a volume of Sabines's love poetry called *Poesía amorosa*—the book you hold in your hands.

Jaime Sabines Gutiérrez was born in 1926 in Tuxtla Gutiérrez, Chiapas, to a Lebanese immigrant father who arrived in Mexico from Cuba, and a Chiapan mother. Beginning with the slim volume *Horal* in 1950 and concluding with *Otros poemas sueltos* (Other Assorted Poems) (1973-1993), Sabines published ten collections of poetry—selections from seven of which constitute this book—works that have been translated into many languages and that earned him widespread critical acclaim and virtually all of his country's major literary awards and honours.

Curiously, though, for a poet who shunned publicity and studiously avoided conventional intellectual circles, Sabines was a wildly popular figure in his native Mexico, where his rare public appearances drew hundreds of fans, prompting Elena Poniatowska to declare that "he brought poetry to the streets." In an email exchange, Émile Martel, Canadian author, former diplomat, and fellow Sabines translator (into Québécois French), described to me his experience of witnessing the poet perform at the Guadalajara Book Fair in 1995: "During the fair, Sabines had a reading; there was such an overflowing crowd in the lecture hall that the reading was broadcast on large screens and hundreds and hundreds of people gathered to watch him. I remember distinctly mouths moving when he read 'Los amorosos.' A living classic, I thought." As a further indication of Sabines's popularity, "Los amorosos" ("The Lovers"), the title of perhaps his most celebrated poem, also provides the title for a forthcoming Mexican movie inspired by the poet's work and set in his beloved Chiapas.

This enormous popular appeal derives in part from his ability to communicate universal truths in an original and accessible, authentically Mexican colloquial diction (which predates the anti-poetry of Nicanor Parra by many years) utterly without pretensions. By contrast, the poetry of Nobel Prize winner Octavio Paz, while attractive to fellow intellectuals, is regarded by many Mexican readers as abstruse and esoteric, the product of a tenured mind. Dubbed "The Sniper of Literature" by Cuban poet Roberto Fernández Retamar, Sabines writes verse that is shockingly direct, often sardonic and irreverent, at times brutal: "There is a way/ for you to make me/ perfectly happy,/ dearest: drop dead." He can be morbid, and autobiographical to the point where the reader senses instinctively that Sabines the poet and the man are in fact one and the same person. In his introduction to this book in the original Spanish, the Uruguayan poet Mario Benedetti writes: "Sabines opens his intimacy, reveals his contradictions without false modesty... This pleases and shocks the reader... Sabines is almost shameless in his sincerity. His contradictions are not pretences but vital paradoxes, junctions where he confronts heart and soul. This is why they affect us so deeply, why they call to us and give rise to doubts, why they become intersections and perplexities that we feel as our own."

Sabines wrote about everyday themes (love, death, social unrest, existential anxiety), people (*us*—the lovers), and places (hospitals, bars, parks, rooming houses, brothels). For over two decades he earned his living selling cloth in his brother Juan's store in Tuxtla Gutiérrez. He later sold animal feed to buyers in Mexico City before being elected to the federal legislature from 1976 to 1979 and again from 1988 to 1991. But if the quotidian struggles of working life coloured and informed his poems, strangely, for a two-term politician who identified with the ideals of the Cuban Revolution and thought capitalism had failed, he wrote few overtly political poems, and saw no contradiction between his working and his writing lives: "Poetry happens like an accident, a mugging, a love affair, a crime; it happens every day, when, alone, a man's heart begins to think about life."

Beyond being a truly popular poet, he received almost universal critical acclaim for his work. "One of the finest contemporary poets of our language," Octavio Paz said of him as early as 1972; and in 1983, when Sabines received the National Prize for Literature (Mexico's highest literary award), the future Nobel Laureate added, "His intense personal opus is in my view among the most important in Latin America and the Spanish language." José Emilio Pacheco, himself one of Mexico's foremost poets, counted Sabines's poems "among the finest of his language and of his times," while Mario Benedetti regarded him as "one of the indispensable poets, not merely of Mexico, but of all Latin America and the Spanish language."

English-speaking readers, too, have commented on Sabines's achievement. Interviewed by the *New York Times* shortly after Sabines's death, the American poet W. S. Merwin said, "He has a voice completely his own. His poetry is extremely intimate and plain, but powerful, sometimes shockingly powerful. It spoke to anybody." And Philip Levine writes: "His best poems are revelations of truths, odd truths, truths we immediately accept, which we have long suspected as truths but have never before heard articulated."

After tripping on a step in 1989 and shattering a hip, Sabines underwent thirty-five separate operations, each of which resulted in further complications. During this time, he was also diagnosed with cerebral cancer. Such a harrowing ordeal might have killed a person half his age, but he responded with great inner fortitude and dignity, receiving a daily flow of admirers, from the Mexican president to doctoral candidates to awestruck schoolchildren, in his hospital room with courtesy and grace, while raising the spirits of depressed friends with doses of his trademark mordant humour: "I'm the one who's fucked up, and can't walk; quit complaining, assholes!"

Forced to give up his lifelong smoking habit, he slowly recovered his health, and with the aid of a cane was able to walk again. Between 1994 and 1997, he felt sufficiently healthy to accept invitations to participate in literary festivals and conferences in Mexico and abroad—Tampico, Monterrey, New York, Montreal, Guadalajara, Paris, Madrid, Montevideo—more out of curiosity about these places than from any desire to congregate with fellow writers, the majority of whom he found pretentious and self-regarding. His desire to live was stronger than ever, as he explained to a reporter in Spain: "I believe in life, I have undergone thirty-five operations; do you think I have gone through them because I want to die?" But constant pain had dogged and debilitated him. He died at his home in Mexico City on March 19, 1999. He was 72. His wake was attended by Mexican President Ernesto Zedillo, who offered to place his coffin in the Capital's Palacio de Bellas Artes as an official honour. The poet's family declined on the grounds that, characteristically, Sabines had requested a simple funeral.

In Mexico, his books routinely sell out. One of them, *Recogiendo poemas* (Collecting Poems), an earlier selection of his work, sold out a print run of half a million copies. Sabines's work continues to be anthologized and translated at a prodigious rate, and biographies, critical studies, documentaries and movies dedicated to his work and life have begun to appear; bridges, bars, cultural centres, festivals and literary prizes bear his name; and young Mexican musicians are recording his words in a wide variety of musical genres and styles. In Europe—particularly in Bulgaria, Germany, Italy, Portugal and Spain—and in the Americas, too, his fame continues to spread. In the words of Mario Benedetti, I invite you "to enter into the complete *oeuvre* of one of the indispensable poets, not merely of Mexico, but of all of Latin America and the Spanish language."

Colin Carberry

from **HORAL (1950)**

THE DAY

Day broke without her.
It barely stirs.
Remembers.

(My eyes, grown thinner,
dream her.)

Absence is so simple!

On the leaves of time,
the drop of this day
slips, shudders.

I'M NOT SURE ABOUT THIS, but I suppose
that a woman and a man
fall in love some day,
little by little, loneliness starts to set in:
something in their hearts tells them they're alone;
all alone, they enter one another;
they go on-killing one another.

This all happens in silence. The way
the light enters the eye.
Love merges bodies.
In silence, they go on filling one another.

They'll wake up, arm in arm, one day,
thinking they know all there is to be known;
they'll see that they're naked and know.

(I'm not sure about this: I suppose.)

I LIKED WHEN YOU CRIED.

Such tender eyes
over your skirt!

I don't know, but there
were big women, black
waters, from everywhere.

Sister, I want to call you,
in order to copulate roses
and tears with you.

It's true, it hurts like hell,
all that comes to you.
Certainly, it hurts
not having anything.

Sadness, you look lovely
when you hush, just so!
Extract her tears
with a kiss!

Ah, let time turn
you into a statue.

IT'S THE SHADOW OF WATER,

and the echo of a sigh,
trace of a look,
memory of an absence,
nakedness of a woman behind a pane.

She is dead and buried—finger
of the heart, she is your ring—
open mystery,
guileless as a child.

Droplets of light
filled vacant eyes,
and a leafy, winged body
took to the dew.

Take her with your eyes;
fill her now, my love.
She is all yours,
yours like a suicide.

Stones that I sank in the air,
wood I drowned in the river,
look how my heart floats
on her simple body.

PLACE OF LOVE, place in which I've lived
at a distance, you–disregarded,
beloved whom I've silenced, glance I haven't seen,
lie I told myself and didn't believe:
at that moment when each of us, alone,
in tears, hatred, death, loved the other,
I am–who knows if I am, if I ever was!–
loving you, crying for myself, astray.

(This is the last time that I'll love you.
I mean it.)

All that I don't know, and haven't learned,
I've learned here and now, with you.

my heart burgeoned in you;
in you, my grief was wrought.
Sweetheart, my place of refuge,
silence in which I'm tormented.

(When I look in your eyes
I think of a child.)

There are times, times when you're so distant
I tell you everything.

Your heart on your sleeve, your hands,
your lost smile wrapped around a shout,
this your so poor and simple heart renewed,
and this your seeking me in places I've never been:

at times, whatever you do, or don't do,
you do just to be fighting with yourself.

Ghost girl, my sweetheart, girl—look what
nonsense was uttered by my deflated heart.

ENTRESOL

A wardrobe, a mirror, a chair,
no sign of a star, my room, the window,
night the same as ever, and I satiated
by chewing gum, a dream, some hope.
Everywhere you look men are roving,
and in the distance, fog, and the morning.
There are frost-locked trees, hard ground,
fixed fish identical to the water,
nests asleep beneath warm doves.
No woman in sight. I'm hurting.
For days my heart has longed to fall on its knees
before a soft touch or a tender word.
The night is harsh. Slow as the dead,
shadows drag themselves up the walls.
That woman and I were stuck tight with water,
her skin draped over my bones
and my eyes held by her gaze.
We have died many times
at the foot of dawn.
I remember that I remember her name,
her lips, her see-through skirt.
Her breasts are succulent, and from one region
of her body to the other, a vast expanse:
from nipple to nipple one hundred lips and an hour;
from pupil to pupil, a heart and two tears.
I love her down to the depths of every abyss,
until the last flight of the last wing,
when all flesh will no longer be flesh

nor the soul a soul.
It's vital to love. I know that now. I love her.
She's so hard, so warm, so guileless!

Tonight I long for her.
The throb of a violin rises from the street to my bed.
Yesterday I saw two small boys combing their hair
before a shop window stuffed with naked mannequins.
For three years, the train's whistle startled me,
now I know it's just a machine.
There's no better goodbye than the everyday kind
to each thing, in every moment, my blood
fired, pulsing on high.
Homeless blood. A calm night,
Insomnia's tobacco. An empty bed.

I'm heading off somewhere else.
And I'm bringing my hand that's always writing and talking.

MISS X

Miss X, yes, the curvy Miss Ecks,
has crossed my path, at last:
hovering about her brief,
infinite, unsuspecting eyes.
She's as supple and clean
as dawn's tender breeze;
happy, smooth and deep
as grass under water.
She turns sad at times,
with that mural sadness that traces
speedy idols and sketches
troubled spectres on her face.
I think of her as a young girl
inquiring things of an old woman;
like a bewildered little donkey
entering a city, burdened with hay.
There's a grown woman in her, too,
who fills her eyes with sudden fear,
and moves inside her and tears up
her innards with acid tears.
Miss X, yes, who smiles at me
and doesn't want to tell me her name,
has told me now, standing on her shadow,
that she loves me, but doesn't love me.
I let her shake her head left and right,
saying no and no, until she tires of it
and my kiss on her hand leaves a winged
seed to bud serenely beneath her skin.

All day yesterday
the wet light glittered,
and Miss X went out, with a thin
cloak draped over her shoulders, in love.
She was never so girlish, never,
in a time so lovely, so lover-like.
Her hair fell on her brow,
her eyes, and my soul.

I took her by the hand and we walked
the whole of the rainy afternoon.

Ah, Miss X, Miss X, hidden
flower of dawn.

You'll not love her, sir, you don't know how to.
I'll see her tomorrow.

MY HEART EMBARKS from my body to your body
on its last voyage.
Offspring of light,
ageless waters that in you, woman astray, are born.
Come to my thirst. Now.
After everything. Before.
Come to my thirst long savoured
in mouths, scarce well-springs.
I love that rapt harp that lulls wild children
in your womb.
I love that taut moisture that arouses you,
that watery moisture that burns you.
Woman, gentle muscle.
The skin of a kiss between your breasts'
darkened surf
roams in my mouth
and measures blood.
You, too. And it isn't too late.
We can still die in each other's arms:
this no-man's land is yours and mine.
Woman, hatred's tenderness, ancient mother,
poison, flame, absence, bitter,
bitter sea, I want to enter,
penetrate, cross you.
Each cell is female, open country,
parted waters—a thing that opens.
I was born to enter you.
I'm the arrow lodged in the loin of a dying gazelle.

I'm poised to know you,
grain of anguish in a bird's heart.
I'll be upon you, and every woman
everywhere will have a man on top of her.

THE LOVERS

The lovers fall silent.
Love is the finest, the most shuddering,
the most unendurable, silence.
The lovers seek,
they are the ones who relinquish,
those who change, who forget.
Their hearts tell them that what they look for,
what they seek, they will not find.

The lovers go around like lunatics
because they are alone, alone, alone;
yielding, giving themselves up at every turn,
crying because they can't hold on to their love.
Love obsesses them. The lovers live
for today; knowing little else, it's all they can do.
They are always going,
forever heading elsewhere.
They wait—
for nothing, but they wait.
For what they know they'll never find.
Love is a perpetual prolongation,
always the next, no, the following, step.
The lovers are incorrigible,
those who always—good for them!—have to be alone.

With serpents for arms, the lovers
are the hydra of the tale;
their neck-veins, too, swell up, serpent-

like, in order to throttle them.
The lovers cannot sleep,
for if they did the worms would devour them.

They open their eyes in the darkness
and terror seizes them.

They see scorpions beneath the sheets
and their bed floats as though on a lake.

The lovers are mad, stone mad,
forsaken of God and Satan.

Trembling and famished,
the lovers come out of their caves
to hunt ghosts.
They laugh at those who know everything,
at those who love forever, heart and soul,
those who believe in love as in an lamp filled with inexhaust-
ible oil.

The lovers play at gathering water,
at tattooing smoke, at going nowhere;
they play the long, sorrowful game of love.
You don't have to give in;
no one has to give in, they say.
The thought of conforming with anything mortifies them.

Hollowed out (picked clean from one rib to the next),
Death gradually distills behind their eyes,
and they cry and wander, adrift, until daybreak,
when trains and roosters bid their painful farewell.

Sometimes, the smells of damp earth, of women
who sleep, soothed, a hand between their thighs,
of trickling water, and of kitchens, reaches them,
and the lovers begin to sing between pursed lips
a song never learned.
And they go on crying, crying for
this beautiful life.

from **THE SIGN (1951)**

from I. THE SIGN

ON ILLUSION

You wrote on the slab of my heart:
desire.
And I drifted days and days,
crazed and aromatic and sad.

from II. CONVALESCENCE

I WANT TO REST MY HEAD

in your hands: Lord
of smouldering shadow,
I want to rest my heart;
I want to cry my eyes out;
depart weeping, Lord.

Love, I'm weak, puny,
thwarted, tired of loving:
strike me with a blast of air,
heart, throw me away.

On the breeze, at dawn,
when the sun begins to wake,
shed me like a tear,
cry me as I cry.

IN THE OPEN EYES OF THE DEAD

there is a strange, lustrous sheen!
Film of air in the motionless pupil,
shadowy veil, tender light.
Love keeps vigil in the open eyes
of dead lovers.
The eyes are like a coveted,
impenetrable, half-open door.
Why does death defer lovers, entomb
them in a place of silence like the earth?
What is it about the weeping light
in the water of the eye—in that wasting
meniscus of trembling glass?
Guardian angels took them to their breasts;
in their gaze, they breathed their last,
died of their own veins.
Those eyes are like stones
left by a blind hand on the face.
Mystery spirits them away.
Ah, the beguiling sweetness
in the casket of the air that entombs them!

THERE'S NOTHING ELSE. ONLY WOMAN to cheer us,
only woman's eyes to comfort us,
only naked bodies,
territories of which men never tire.
If, in this time of growth, it isn't possible
to dedicate oneself to God,
what can we give the tormented heart
but the circle of necessary death
that is woman?

We are having sex, pure beauty,
heart lonely and clean.

MY LITTLE LOVE, you don't know it,
you can't possibly know it yet:
it's not your voice, the cold angel
of your mouth, nor your responses
to the sandalwood you breathe
and exude, that move me;
neither your ardent,
crucified virgin's stare.

Your eloquently expressed
anguish doesn't move me,
nor does your silent,
hopeless weeping.

Your melancholy gestures
don't move me;
nor your longing, your hope,
nor the wound
of which you talk, tormented.

It's your entire being—
your depicting your life
with such ungainly, cleansing
passion, that moves me,
like he who wants to kill himself
to be able to say: I'm a suicide.

Leaf that hardly stirs
and already feels stricken:
I'm going to keep loving you
all day long.

SOURCE OF SORROW, your
black pupils brand
and berate me. Your lips,
despite you, kiss me.
How you've sustained
that same dark look
with these eyes
trained on me now!

You smiled. What silence,
what lack of rejoicing!
How I sought you
out in your smile,
head of earth,
sad lips!

You don't cry, you wouldn't,
even if you wanted to;
your face has the burned-out look
of the blind.

You can laugh; I allow you
to, even though you can't.

CLOSED UP, SEALED OFF,

lonely and sad and sick,
tall and slim, silently
grieving, beautiful.

You can't tell from that look
if she looks or remembers.
(if she's mourning a loved one,
or has murdered and is reflecting.)

She's as sweet, as sour,
as distant and as close
to you as she is
to herself.

Unhappy young woman,
confidante, stranger,
you're so dead that when you die
no one will ever be able to tell.

HER EYES WERE IN SHADOW,
and her eyes were blank
and fearful, sweet and good
and cold.

There were her eyes and they were
in her shy and natural face
and her face made them
calm.

Unlooking and looking, so lonely
and tender with fright, so mine,
leaving her mouth on my lips
they cried a lost air,
ungrieving and open and absent
and distant, distant and hurt
in the shadow in which they were, they were
shy, vacant.

And a girl in her eyes all alone
without anything met mine
and she fell silent, looked, and fell silent
and her eyes wide open and clear,
waterstone gazing at me
beyond my childless eyes
and so lonesome they were, and so sad,
so clear.

And in the shadow shrouding her eyes
and afflicted in unpeopled air,
there were her eyes, and they were
vacant.

HOW PLEASING THIS CONTACT with your eyes,
light as startled doves at the edge of the water!
How quick they are to make contact
with my gaze!

Who are you? It doesn't matter!
Despite yourself,
in your eyes a brief, enigmatic
word.
What, I don't wish to know. I love
your sidelong, shy, startled glances at me.
That way I think you are fleeing from something:
from me or from you; from nothing;
from those temptations they say torment married women.

AT THE AIR'S FRINGE
(what do we say or do?)
there's still a woman.

In the wilderness, stretched
out on the grass,
if we look closely:
a woman.

Under the water, in the water,
open, light up your eyes:
look at her with care.

Algae, schools of fish,
castaways' eyes,
fronds of tea, sing to her,
look at her with care.

In mines, lost, slender,
and shadow too,
veins of dark silver
satisfy her thirst.

Behind you, wherever you are,
if you turn around quickly
you'll see her.

In the air, hidden like a leaf
in a tree, there is always
a woman.

YOU UNDRESS AS YOU WOULD if you were alone
and suddenly you discover that you're with me.
O how I love you then
between the sheets and the cold!

You begin flirting with me as if I were a stranger
and I, demure, half-heartedly play along.
I think that I'm your husband
and that you're cheating on me with me.

And the love we make then in the laughter
of finding ourselves alone in forbidden love!

(Then, when it's over, I'm afraid of you
and a chill runs up my spine.)

from III. THE WORLD

I'VE SEEN THEM AT THE MOVIES,

outside the theatres,
on trams and in parks,
hands clasped and eyes closed.
Girls in darkened movie theatres offering
their breasts to hands,
opening their lips for a wet kiss
and parting their legs for invisible satyrs.
I've seen them love each other hastily, imagining
the pleasure their dresses conceal, the ruse
of the tender word that desires,
strangers each to each.
It's the flower that blooms
on the longest day,
the heart that shakes
like a blind man in the grip of a premonition.

She was fourteen years old, that girl I saw
today, her parents beside her watching
her laughter as though she had stolen it.

I have often seen them
—*them*, the lovers—
on pavements, on the grass, beneath trees,
touching each other,
sealing their love with kisses.
And I have seen the black sky
emptied even of birds,
steel structures

and shabby houses, backyard lots,
forgotten places.
And they, forever true, tremble,
hold each other tight,
and love smiles, excites, instructs them,
like an old grandfather who is beyond illusions.

AFTER ALL—and I mean after all—
it's only about going to bed together,
it concerns the flesh,
naked bodies,
the lantern of death in this world.

Decapitated glory, time's
deaf-mute survivor,
meagre wages of those who die together.

Eternity, you damned the quest
for pleasure to misery; to thirst,
you chained undeserved failure;
the heart you nailed to a wall.

It's about my body that I bless,
against which I struggle,
that must give me all it has,
in a powerful silence
and that dies and kills frequently.

Solitude, brand me with your bare foot,
squeeze my heart like grapes,
fill my mouth with its aged spirits.

ANOTHER LETTER

You're always by my side and for this I thank you.
When anger consumes me, or when I'm sad
—daubed with the balm of sorrow as though I
were dying—
you seem removed, untouchable, beside me.
You gaze on me like a child, and I forget everything
and then I love you happily, excruciatingly.
I've brooded on God's longevity,
on the lard and sulphur of madness,
and on all that I've witnessed in my brief life.
You are like the milk of this world.
I know you: you're with me more than I am.
What else can I offer you but heaven?
The poets have given the moon a thousand names—
Medallion, God's eye, Silver Globe,
Coin of Honey, Woman, Drop of Air—
but the moon in the sky is just the moon,
indefatigable, miraculous, like you.
Sometimes I want to cry out of sheer rage,
for what I don't know, for some reason,
because it's impossible to own you, or anything;
to cease being alone.
With the joy derived from writing a poem,
or the tenderness that trembles in the hands of the elderly,
you draw close to me and you shape me
in the scales of your eyes,
in the magic formula of your hands.
A doctor has told me that I have a heart like a drop

—elongated like a drop—and I believe him,
because I feel like a dank cave into
which I'm always dropping, revivifying, dropping
always.

Blessed are you amongst all women,
you, who don't bother me:
like a paraplegic's wheelchair, a blind man's cane,
you are always close at hand.
Virgin even to he who possesses you,
enduring mystery to the man who knows you,
what more can I give you but hell?
From the swell of your breasts
my face is slowly drowning in,
I run my eye along you, to the tips of your toes,
where the world begins.
You have donned your skin of woman,
womanly softness and moist organs,
thawed statue into which I sweetly enter,
melted hands with which you touch the fever that I am,
and the chaos I am preserves you.
My Death drifts above us both,
and you draw me from Her like water from a well,
water for God's thirst that I am then,
water for the raging fire of God that I feed.

When the empty hour strikes
you know how to work your fingers like a balm,
couch them on my downy eyes,
laugh with your finger-tips.

What else can I give you but the earth?
Embedded in the dung of days,
I watch my love flourish, like trees
that no one has climbed and whose shade
dries the grass, and makes men feverish.

Flawed, mortal, guileless daughter
of men,
I usurp you daily, that I know,
your mercy makes use of me all the time,
and you love me, and then I'm
like the child we always wanted.

I want to talk about you continuously
in a conference of the deaf,
to show your image to every blind man I meet.
I want to give you to no one
so you'll come back to me without having left.

In the parks, where birds gather and sunlight
flecks the fallen leaves and one sweetly yearns for
the old maids tenderly eyeing children,
I desire, I dream of you.
The longing I feel for you when you're not elsewhere!
(Let's eat some grapes this afternoon,
or, if it rains, drink coffee,
and be together always, forever, until night descends.)

from **ADAM & EVE (1952)**

I

—We were in paradise. Nothing ever happens in paradise. We didn't know each other. Eve, get up.

—I'm in love. I'm tired, and hungry. Has the sun come up yet?

—It has, but there are still a few stars. The sun in the distance is moving towards us and the trees are breaking into a gallop. Listen.

—I feel like biting your jaw-bone. Come, I'm naked, pummelled, and I smell of you.

Adam moved towards her and he took her. And it seemed as if they both had walked into a very broad river, and that they were playing up to their necks in water, and laughing, while the little mixed-up fish nipped at their legs.

II

Last night was a night of magic. There are drums in the night, and the animals sleep with their sense of smell open like an eye. Nothing stirs in the air. Leaves and feathers gather in the boughs, on the ground, and sometimes somebody moves them, and they fall silent. Black rags, black voices, thick black silences drift, drag along, and the earth puts on its black visage and grimaces at the stars.

Hearts thump, beat hard, when they feel the wing of terror glide near, and every eye warns that things move in the same spot forever.

At night, no one can take a step. Whoever enters the thicket of the night with open eyes gets lost, attacked by shadow, and nothing more will be known of him. Like those whom the sea has chosen.

—Eve, said Adam, quietly, let's not separate.

III

—Have you noticed how the plants grow? At the spot where the seed drops, the water appears: it's the water that germinates, climbs towards the sun. Through the trunk and the branches, it rises into the air, as when you stare into the noon sky and your eyes begin to glisten.

The plants grow from one day to the next. It's the earth that grows; it turns soft, green, and pliant. The mouldy clod of soil and the bark of the old trees crumble, return.

Have you noticed this? The plants move in time, not from one place to the next: from one hour to the next. You can feel it when you stretch out on the ground, face up, and your hair reaches down like a clump of roots, and your whole body is like a fallen tree-trunk.

—I want to plant a seed in the river to see if a floating tree that I can climb and play on will grow. The fish would tangle themselves in its foliage, and it would be a water tree that would go everywhere without ever falling.

IV

—Yesterday I was observing the animals and I began to think about you. Females are smoother, softer, and more dangerous. Before they surrender to the male, they abuse him, they flee; they defend themselves. Why? I've seen this in you, too: you flare up, like the doves, when I'm at ease. Is it that your blood and mine ignite at different times?

Now that you're sleeping you should answer me. Your breathing's calm, your features are relaxed, your lips open. You could tell me everything without getting distressed, without giggling.

Is it that we're different? But weren't you made from my side? Doesn't it hurt you?

When I'm inside you, when I make myself small and you hold me, grip me, close around me like a flower around an insect, I know something. We know something. The female is always greater, in some way.

We save each other from death. How come? Every night we save each other. We lie together, in one another's arms, and I begin to grow like the day.

I have to go looking for something in you, something of mine that you are that you'll never give me.

Why did they separate us? I need you, like a third eye, like another leg that only I know I had, in order to walk and to see.

V

—Look, this is our house; this, our roof. Against the rain, against the sun, against the night, I built it. The cave won't move and animals are always trying to get in. It's different here, and we're different as well.

—Different, because we defend ourselves, Adam? I think we're weaker.

—We are different because we want to change. We are better.

—I don't want to be better. I think we're losing something. I think we're separating ourselves from the wind. Among all the earth's creatures, we'll be the strangest. Remember the first skin you threw over me: you removed my skin; you made it useless. We're going to end up being different from the stars, and we'll no longer understand even the trees.

—That's because we have something called a soul.

—We're more and more afraid, Adam.

—You'll see. We will know. Never mind that our body...

—Our body?

—...is thinner. We're intelligent—capable of more.

—What are you thinking? That day you sat under the tree of the evil shadow your head was hurting you. Does it still hurt? I'm going to bury you up to your knees again.

VI

—The trunk was burning after the rain went away. The lightning-bolt subdued him and sank into him. Now he's tame lightning. We'll take care of him here, and offer him leaves and grass to eat. I like the fire. Approach him slowly, with your hand outstretched, and he'll caress you or he'll burn you: you know how far your friendship goes.

—I like him because he's red, blue, and yellow; and he floats in the air and has no shape. And when he wants to sleep he hides in the ashes and watches you from within with his little red eyes. So charming! Then he'll get up and begin to forage, and if he finds a branch nearby, he'll devour it. I like him, I do; I really like him! I'll take care of him, he's no bother, and so humble!

—He's proud, but he's good. What's wrong with you? You have remained...

—Nothing.

—Your eyes are open and you're sleeping. Are you listening to me? He has sunken himself into you as well. I can see him, coiled, like a snake, in the depths of your eyes, enamouring you. You remain still while he runs through you, covetously. You revolve around the fire without moving.

Unequivocal, lingering fire, continual tree, your instantaneous leaves and enduring trunk entice us. Let us be with you, together with your ravenous love. You grow by obliterating: means of destruction, inward stature, outward endurance, inverted time, dying death, birth.

Let us be in your flickering eyelids, to seek with you whatever it is that you seek, light in perpetual flight, in you, like you yourself, inside us.

VII

—What's the song of the birds, Adam?

—It's the birds themselves made into air. To sing is to spill yourself out into drops, into threads of air; it is to tremble.

—That's when the birds are ripe, when their throats turn into leaves, and their leaves are smooth, piercing, and sometimes quick. Why, though? Why is it I have not ripened?

—When you are ripe you are going to shed yourself, and the part of you that is fruit will rejoice, and the part of you that is branch will go on trembling. Then you will know. The sun has yet to enter into you like the day. You are awakening.

—I feel like singing. I have this air, part-bird and part-me, trapped inside me. I am going to sing.

—You are always singing without realizing it. You are like the water. The stones don't realize either, and their lime quietly gathers and sings silently.

VIII

"Three days ago Adam went out, and he hasn't come back. Oh, I was happy, I was happy.

"I've been terrified; I haven't been able to sleep.

"I'm alone. Why won't he come back? I went looking for him, I called out to him, but he was nowhere to be found. The night frightens me. What can I do without him? Everything's so big, so long, and so futile. I'm lost, and surrounded by strange things. Why hasn't he come back?

"Adam, Adam, Adam, the fire's going out, *I'm* about to go out, and you won't come back. What are you going to find?"

And Eve fell asleep. And she was sleeping when Adam arrived.

Adam arrived tired, but he didn't rest. He began to watch her, and he was seeing her for the first time.

IX

The shadow of the banana tree is so cool! From a single banana leaf, innumerable drops of water break loose and are forever falling. I love the green, fluted leaves, the banana bunches, and the sharp, singular shoots, like a school of fish drifting upwards. Look at the trunk: it's a honeycomb of water!

I love the banana grove and its shady, low-lying humidity, its bed where the sun rots, and its battered, tranquil leaves. I love the banana grove when it rains, because of the musical sounds it makes, because it grows happy like a leaping animal bathing itself.

I love the shadow of the banana tree, its little nests of air, and the fragrant, sleepy air learning to fly. I love to throw myself down on the rootless earth, feel the flow of the water and lie motionless, listening.

X

We went to the sea. What fear and happiness I felt! It's an enormous, restless animal. Always frightening, it thrashes and blows, by turns calm and furious. It seemed as though it was watching us from deep beneath the water's surface with its countless eyes: eyes like those we have in the heart for seeing into the distance or the darkness.

In the beginning, it knocked us over numerous times. Then Adam flew into a fury and started lashing out at the waves. From my vantage point on the beach, I watched, laughing. Adam wasn't up to it. He came out after a while, tired and sweating, and without saying a word, fell asleep.

Then I began to listen to the sea. It was getting dark. With its deep voice, and its vast, unending silence, it sounds like the night. It projects its dark noise, penetrating us through every pore. It sounds like dense water, water that like a badly wounded animal wants to get up.

From now on we're going to live at the edge of the sea. Here the sun and the sea are at the same level, at the same depth as the stars and the big fish.

We'll learn from the sea. He too has his mountains, his vast plains, his birds and his minerals, and his singular and tangled vegetation. We'll study his moods, his seasons, and his endurance in the world like an enormous root: the root of the tree of water that girds the land, immense tree that extends itself into space forever.

The sea is good and terrible, like my father. I want to call him Father Sea. Father Sea, sustain me; beget me anew in your heart. Render me imperishable, receiver of the world, purifier no matter what.

XI

My body aches, my eyes sting, it feels as though I were on fire. My life-blood's boiling inside me. And an icy cold breeze scurries hurriedly beneath my skin, driving my jaw-bone upwards with incessant, jolting blows.

I'm burning alive, I can't even move, I'm weak, wounded, and frightened. Eve hasn't slept; she's petrified, and has placed leaves on my brow. Last night, when I started talking she threw herself on me, rubbed against me, and tried to hush me. There she was, with her eyes as wet as my back. I told her that her eyes hurt me as well and she pressed them against my mouth.

I'm thirsty now, battered and dried-out. In pain. My head is mashed like a rotten fruit. There isn't a part of me that isn't fighting with another. I want to clench my fists. This is all so strange for me!

This is being someone else; some other Adam. He's passing through me, and it's killing.

I'd like to be surrounded by burning rocks.

The other day a tree caught my eye, and I struck it down. It fell with a breaking, collapsing noise. That's just how I sound: struck down, hemmed in, shattered; resounding.

XII

It's a huge, smouldering, black rock, harder than the others. It looks like a lair of lightning bolts. It toppled some trees and shook the ground. It's one of those fiery ones we've seen fall in the distance —they drop from the sky like ripe oranges, they're swift, and they last longer in your eyes than in the air. This one's rough, scorching, and retains the sky's cold colour.

I like to see them drop so fast, swifter than birds shot from the sky. There has to be a place up above where they die and where they fall from. Some of them must fall forever. They seem to travel a great distance, but where to?

—This one came here. But I'm going to move it somewhere else. I'll roll it into the bamboo trees, and it'll demolish them. I want it to cool down so that I can crack it open.

—Crack it open! What if a flock of stars come out, and they take off? They're apt to rush out in a racket like flushed quails.

XIII

Eve is no longer here. Just like that, she stopped talking. She remained quiet and stiff. At first I thought she was sleeping. Then I felt her and her skin had gone cold. I moved her; I spoke to her, and left her lying there.

Days went by and she didn't get up. She began to reek. She was rotting like a fruit, and swarming with flies and ants. She was in rough shape.

I dragged her outside and covered her with piles of straw. Every day, I would check to see how she was. Until I grew tired, and carried her farther away. She never spoke again. She was like a dried branch.

She does nothing, she's useless. Little by little, the earth devours her. There she lies.

The sun consumes her. I don't like her like this. She won't get up, won't speak; won't grow.

I've been watching her. It's futile. There's less of her, every day she weighs less. She's finished.

XIV

Ah, you, still, sleeping protector of the world, pregnant with Death. It's pointless my talking to you, or to myself!

Man alone I am, I'm left behind. One-armed, pruned, sliced open, I'll stay.

I'll die here. For Death has me in her sights, and hovers around me, hunting me, dragging me away. I'll say no more now. I'm not moving from this spot.

XV

Nightly, under my hands, these hands that measure it, kiss it, rub it over and over, beneath my eyes that stay watching it the whole night through, your mild, smooth, inexhaustible womb grows sweetly.

I notice too that your breasts grow, filled with you, round and sagging. And there's something different about you: you laugh; and you have this distant look.

My child is making you sweeter, tenderer. You voice sounds like the foot of a dove cracking open.

Protector, I'll safeguard you from all ghosts; cleave to you, so that you may ripen in peace.

from **WEEKLY DIARY AND POEMS IN PROSE (1961)**

I REJOICE THAT THE SUN HAS COME OUT after so many hours: I rejoice that the trees are stretching like someone getting out of bed; I rejoice that the cars have gasoline and that I have love; I rejoice that this is the 26th day of the month; I rejoice in the fact that we're still alive.

I rejoice that there are sad people, like this girl who could love me if she wasn't in love with someone else. I rejoice in the goodness of God that He allows me to rejoice.

Ding! Dong! I am happy: I want to do everything: not to intoxicate myself with this glass of tequila, but to heal my soul; stand on my hands to make you laugh; stick out my tongue and make your belly ache.

I bite you under your ear, salivate on your left nipple, and I know for certain that I'm close to your heart.

Look, day: let's be good friends. I won't give anyone a thing. I'll be generous: I'll kneel in a corner and stretch out my hands, so that the sun, a man passing by, girls on their way to school, and the little old ladies coming from church will toss me a coin. Like the convict fresh out of jail, I want to be good.

Bottoms up, skeletons!

IS IT THAT WE DO THINGS just to remember them? Do we live merely to have memories of our lives? For it happens that even hope is memory and desire the recollection of that which is to come.

Paradise lost will always be paradise! In the shadow of our souls our bodies met and made love. They loved each other with the love that has no words, which holds only kisses; a love that leaves no trace of itself, for it's like the shadow of a cloud, the light and fresh shadow in which the roses open.

Pure sex, pure love: free of tricks and ambushes. Zeal of the lonely body that plays at dying—the laughter of both, like that of water and of children; laughter of the animal in the laughing rain.

On your skin you still bear the trace of my desire, and my body is embedded in yours, like that of sweat and of smell.

Where are we, Eve and Adam, after so many centuries of calling each other by so many names? We are here, lying on this bed of grass, in the seething wind of bolted windows, under all the stars of the darkened room.

IF I WERE TO DIE within the next couple of minutes, I'd write these wise words: tree of bread and honey, rhubarb, Coca-Cola, Zonite, swastika. And I'd burst into tears.

You can even cry to the word "toilet" if you feel like crying...

And that is how it is with me today. I'm willing to lose even my nails, to gouge out my eyes and squeeze them like lemons over a cup of coffee. ("Wouldn't you like a nice cup of coffee with little peels of eye, my dear.")

Before the icy silence falls on my tongue, before my throat is slit and my heart implodes like a leather bag, I want to tell you, dearest, how grateful I am for this amazing liver that allowed me to devour all your roses the day I entered your hidden garden without anyone seeing me.

I remember. I filled my heart with diamonds—those aged and fallen stars in the dust of the earth—and I was banging it like a baby-rattle while I laughed. I hold no grudge except for the one I hold, and that's because I could have been born before and you didn't do it.

Don't put love in my hands like a dead bird.

THE TONSILS KNOCK YOU OUT like pneumonia, you say,
and you claim that illness is a cudgel in the hands
of a blind man.

We fear knowing too much.

Now the roses of the sky let their petals drop
silently. This declining light is a caress.

I recall that you kiss as if you were nibbling grapes.
No dove like you had turned into a woman until now.

I've liked thinking of you, ever since I learned to think.

THERE IS A WAY
for you to make me
perfectly happy,
dearest: drop dead.

from **ASSORTED POEMS (1951-1961)**

YOUR BODY BY MY SIDE

is soft, sweet, silent.
Your eyes are closed
and your head is resting on my chest,
my gaze travels over you and I smoke
and tousle your loving hair.
This finite tenderness that mutes me
is wrapping its arms around you while
mine remain motionless.
I watch my body, the thigh
on which your weariness rests,
your soft breast hidden, pressed,
your belly breathing slow and smooth
bereft of my lips.
In hushed tones, I tell you
things I make up continuously
and I get truly sad and lonely
and kiss you as if you were your image.
Without speaking, you gaze at me
and you cling to me and cry
tearlessly, eyelessly, fearlessly.
And I light another cigarette while everything
in the room begins to listen to what we do not say.

YOU HAVE ME IN YOUR HANDS

and you read me like an open book.
You're privy to what I overlook,
and you tell me the things I keep from myself.
I learn more from you than from me,
you're like a miracle with no end,
a sorrow with no source.
If you weren't female, we'd be friends.
Sometimes I want to talk of the women
whom I pursue under your nose.
You're like forgiveness
and I'm like your son.
Ah, the beauty of your eyes when we're together!
How distant and abstracted you look
when I abandon you to solitude!
As sweet as your name, like a fig,
you await me in your love until I arrive.
You are like my house,
you're like my death, my dear.

LET'S STORE THIS DAY
among the hours, forever.
This darkened room,
Debussy and the rain,
you next to me, resting after love.
Thick, entranced smoke from my cigarette
drifting through your hair like a caressing hand.
Your back like a prairie in the silence,
and your side an unmoving slope
from which my kisses try to rise, as though out of a dream.

The airless room hangs heavy with love, with fatigue,
with your virgin heart hating me and hating you.
All this discomfiture of sex gratified,
this healing seeking of each other's eyes
in a shadowed no-man's land
of reconciliation.
Your stony-faced look, last mask
in which, despite yourself, you sought sanctuary,
in which you tamed your solitude.
The two of us, our souls renewed, wondering why.
And later your hand squeezing mine,
your head lightly resting on my chest,
and my fingers whispering who knows what to your neck.
Let's store this day
forever among the hours.

YOU HAVE WHAT I'M AFTER, what I long for; whatever
it is I love, you're it.
The fist of my heart is pounding, pleading.
Thanks be to the fairy tales for you.
I thank your mother and your father,
and Death, for not having laid eyes on you.
Thanks be to the air for you.
You are slim as a wisp of wheat,
and delicate, like the outline of your body.
I have never loved a slender woman
but you have enamoured my hands,
tethered my lust,
lured my eyes like two fish.
So here I am at your door, waiting.

LUSTED AFTER, FORBIDDEN,

you're but a step away, enchantress.
With your eyes, you give yourself to passing men,
to he who covets your melting ripeness,
who begs for your body as for his grave.
Wicked, young, horny,
untouched virgin,
I'm watching and loving you
and your fiery blood,
your turning, bobbing head,
your body supine upon the grapes and the smoke.
You're perfect, coveted.
I love you and your mother when you're together.
She's still beautiful and has
knowledge not yet yours.
I don't know which I prefer
when she fixes your dress
and releases you to look for love.

I'M NOT DYING OF LOVE: I'm dying of you,
my love—dying of the love of you,
of my dire need for my skin of you,
of my soul and my mouth of you,
of the miserable wretch I am without you.

I'm dying of you and me, of both
of us, of this–
ripped to shreds, torn apart,
the two of us are dying, dying of it.

We're dying in my room where I'm alone,
on my bed where you're missing,
in the streets where my arm goes unaccompanied,
at the movies and in parks, on trams,
in places where your head rested on my shoulder,
and my hand held yours,
and all of you I know like myself.

We die in places lent to air
so that you can be away from me,
and go to airless enclaves where
I cover you with my skin
and we come to know each other in ourselves,
unworlded, joy-saturated, without end.

We're dying, this we know, ignore, we are dying
together, now, sundered
each from the other, daily,

moulded into multiple statues,
in gestures we don't see,
in our hands that need us.
We're dying, love, I'm dying in your womb
that I neither nibble nor kiss,
in your sweet and living thighs,
and in your unending flesh, I'm dying of masks,
and of dark and incessant triangles.
I'm dying of your body and of mine,
of our death, love, I, we, are dying.
In love's pit at all hours,
inconsolable, in sobs and screams
inside me, I mean to say, I call you,
those who are being born, who are coming from
behind, from you, those who reach you, are calling you.
We are dying, love, and, hour by hour,
we do nothing but die a little more,
and write and talk to each and die together.

HERE YOU'RE ALONE and I'm alone.
You do your daily chores and you think,
and I think, I reminisce, and I'm alone.
At the same instant, we both recall something,
and we suffer. We're like a drug that's equal parts
you and me; and a cellular madness,
a ceaseless insurgent blood courses through us.
This lonely body will break out in sores;
strip by strip, my flesh will fall.
This is bleach and death.
Abrasive being: this dying
disease is the death of us.

I don't know where you are. I've already forgotten
who or where you are, what your name is.
I'm only a part, only an arm,
barely a half, merely a limb.
My mouth and my hands remember you.
With my tongue, eyes, hands, I know you:
you taste like love, sweet love, and flesh,
ploughing, flower; you smell of love and of you.
You smell like salt, you taste like salt, love and me.
On my lips I know, I sense you,
and you turn, you are, you seem inexhaustible
and your whole being
beats inside my heart like my blood.
I tell you that I'm alone, that I miss you.
We miss each other, love, and we're dying
and we'll do nothing else but die.

This I know, love; we both know it.
Today and tomorrow, yes, and when we're
in one another's pure and weary arms,
I'll miss you, love; we'll miss each other.

IT STRIKES ME THAT I MISS YOU,

that I seek you out in crowds, amidst the noise,
but it's all in vain.
When I'm alone
I'm lonelier—alone
everywhere and for you and me.
I do nothing but wait.
Wait the whole day for you to arrive.
Until I fall asleep
and you're nowhere to be found,
and, terribly weary,
I fall asleep again,
wondering.
Love, every single day,
here by my side, next to me, I miss you.
You could begin reading this
and when you arrive begin reading anew.
Close these words like a circle,
like a ring: spin it; set it on fire.
These things flit around me like flies,
and in my throat like flies in a jam-jar.
I am laid waste to my bones:
all is grief.

SONGS FROM THE DRY WELL

1

Spin in the song of your laugh,
knock it down, heart,
throw it to the sun, taking your time,
heart.
Throw off your death,
your mourning,
my lucky love,
ghost of fright.
In this *son* cum rum—
agony's joy—
drink it down, my love,
and lie down all day.
It's getting hot
(who makes it so?)
Make yourself, drum,
mouth of the echoing chasm,
love, nugget of gold,
make yourself hot.
spill your hot blood
on my forehead.
Heart, keep quiet,
so you don't startle
fearful unwanted hope;
throw yourself, love, over my life.
And dance the *son* with me,
and sing it so I may sing it,

meanwhile, heart,
come with me.

2

Aguamarine, the ungrateful
stone that doesn't kill.
Skywater, water of jasmine,
has come late
but has finally come.
Skywater from the East
and the other. Crushed stone.

Slum water, water
of the jaundiced eye,
nitric acid of death:
my sweetheart.
Blue green yellow water,
water of a shattered star,
here at your shore
is my gaze.
(Using words to say
nothing is so tasty!)

3

Sing whenever you're sad,
and cry when you're happy.
When you're down, really
down, go take a look around.
What wall can hold back song?
No force can keep you
from earth or cloud
when you sing.

Few words are needed to sing;
put one in your mouth and play
as if with a stone or a sweet
between tooth, tongue and palate.
When you grasp this, you'll be free
of fright and anxiety.

Come, my love, sing,
(ring-ring-ring-ring)
and I'll be watching.

4

My days flit past
like the shadows of birds.
I'm tired of living.
My heart is a hunger forgotten.
Life slips away

like sand through your fingers,
and the earth blooms with flowers and children.
My dream is to love,
to sing in my sleep, as if to be born,
or to die.

5

Tonight we're going to let loose.
The music you want,
the drink of your choice,
and any woman you like.
Tonight we'll dance.
Blessed desire stretches
like a cat in a haversack;
it's in your blood, poised to strike
like a hunter hidden in scrub.
Tonight we'll get blind drunk.
Sweet alcohol fires your body
with a little flame of immortality,
and fig, grape, and honey
fuse their spirits together.
Tonight we'll fall in love.
God brought mortal woman
into the world—
the serpent-snake of land and sea—
the best thing the Old Man ever did!
Tonight we're going to let loose!

IT ISN'T YOUR BODY,

your skin, eyes, or womb,
or that secret place we know so well,
our death's quagmire, our grave's dead end.
It isn't your mouth—your mouth
which is like your sex—
your breasts' perfect symmetry,
your smooth and delightful back,
or your belly, from which I drink.
It isn't your thighs, hard as day,
your knees of fired ivory,
your diminutive, flagrant feet,
your aroma, nor your hair.
It isn't your gaze—what's a gaze?—
sad, stray light, disembodied peace,
it isn't the book of your ear, your voices, the dark
bags that sleep leaves beneath your eyes.
It isn't your serpent-like tongue either,
dart of wasps through the blind air,
nor the sultry moistness of your asphyxia
that bears your kiss.
It has nothing—not a breeze,
petal, drop, grain, or instant—
to do with your body:
It's purely where you were once
in these my stubborn arms.

WE'RE HERE TOGETHER

again in this house as in Noah's Ark:
Blanca, Irene, María and the others,
Jorge, Eliseo, Óscar and Rafael...
Let's quickly get to know one another,
fornicate and forget each other.
Ox, Tiger, Dove, Alligator and Ass, we all
drink it up, trample on and barge into each another
at this hour poised to plunge into the night's deluge.
Alcohol-flashes streak the darkness of the pupils,
and thunderclaps and music clash with naked voices.
The house turns and sets sail for the wee hours.
Who's holding your hand, Magdalena, under the pillows?
What a lovely profession you have, to undress
and illuminate the room!
Make love, my little dove, with all the skill
your trained hands, mouth and eyes,
your expert heart, can muster!
Salomé, here is the day's head
so you can dance before the host of blazing eyes.
Lesbia, don't take even a petal from our hands!
The house ascends with the whirlpool and time rises
like bitter flour. Here we all are, stewed to the gills,
our souls spilling from our every pore!

IN THE MOUTH OF THE BONFIRE burn my days,
the dead leaves and dry grass that I am.
My soul feels like scorched earth.
Eyes: see nothing but the everyday ghosts.
Mouth: say nothing but the greeting, "Good evening,"
and, for weather: "A fine evening," or "It's pouring rain."
Hands and fingers: go on gripping the desk,
the wine-glass, banknotes, and thighs.
Sole of my foot: you must walk the beaten path,
alongside the same cars, over the same ants.
Heart: devote yourself to your blood, and my lungs.
And you, dear stomach: digest whatever I fill you with.
Millwheel: we're no strangers.
For you, my most beloved, most hated, I'll be seeking out
the sweetest names
and secreting them in your ear with my tongue.
I want to fill your head with that foam of the sea.
I'm no good for anything but the birds.
God, my tree: let me fall from you like your shadow.

from **YURIA (1967)**

from II. TOYSHOP AND SONGS

EMPTY STOMACH: LIGHT HEART. Let's sing to the hot cup of coffee, to the maligned cigarette, to carcinogenic, heavenly Bach, at this righteous hour of solitude.

Let's learn to make love as the doves do. Let's cry like children. There is still time to rise alongside the sun.

Cloying, worn-out, night descends. I'm going to lie dead in the curve of your back for a while—on your back, on your sleep-suffused body, over your motionless arms, and your breasts that breathe in my hands—oh absent one.

For throughout all these days I have longed to love you, but the time of our love has run out.

I HOPE TO BE CURED OF YOU one of these days. I have to quit smoking you, drinking you, thinking you. It's possible, following the moral guidelines of our times. I prescribe time, abstinence, solitude.

Would you mind if I loved you for only a week? It's neither too much nor too little. It's plenty. In a week one can gather up all the words of love that have ever been uttered and set them ablaze. I'm going to ignite you with this bonfire of burned-out love. And silence too. Because the finest words of love are between two people who say nothing.

We will have to burn this other lateral and subversive language of the lover as well. (You know I am really telling you I love when I say: "It's getting hot," "Give me water," "Do you know how to drive?", "Night has fallen"... Among the people, in the midst of your folks and mine, I have said to you, "It is late," and you knew that I was saying, "I love you.")

One week more to gather up all the love of time. To give it to you. So you can do whatever you want with it: keep it, caress it, throw it away. It serves no purpose, that much is certain. I only want one week to figure things out. Because this is a lot like leaving a lunatic asylum to enter a graveyard.

I SAY LOVE CAN'T BE SAID.

Love is eaten like bread,
it is chewed like a lip,
drunk like water from a well.
Love is grieved like a death,
relished like a disguise.
Love hurts like a welt,
hums like a honeycomb,
it's as tasty as a grape,
and like life it is mortal.

Love simply cannot be said,
with or without words.
The wind tries to say it
and the ocean's rehearsing it.
But the lover has it as ingrown
as a blood-bathed mole,
and love is like a burning coal
and a touch of salt.

An amputee's hand can touch it,
the mute tongue, the eyes of a blind man,
say it and see it.
There's no cure for love
and it only wants to play.

MY LOVE, MY DEAR, love suddenly
found in the oyster of death,
I want to eat with, be, love with you,
touch and watch you.

I tell myself, the blood pulsing
through my veins tells me,
and this pain and my shoes,
mouth and pillow, tell me so.

I love you, my dear love, absurdly,
foolishly, all lit up, head over heels,
rose-dreaming, conjuring stars; saying
goodbye to you walking beside you.

I love you from the pole on the corner,
from the carpet of that empty room,
on the warm sheets of your body
where a vase of poppies sleeps.

Long hair of the restless air,
river of night, dark banana grove,
blind beehive, unearthed love,

I'll follow your footsteps upwards,
from your feet to your thigh to your rib.

YOU ARE MY HUSBAND, and I am your wife.
You are my sister and I your brother.
You are my mother and I am your son.
The two of us are nothing, if not one.

You open yourself, I penetrate you.
You are Mary and I am Joseph.
You grip me; I wrap my arms around you.
You are my blood and I am your skin.

Carmen and Rosa, Berta and Beatriz,
Carlos and Pedro, Jorge and Rubén,
you are the glass, the water, the stone,
the charcoal, the vinegar, the honey.

I am your mouth, hand, and navel,
ear and tongue, nail and foot.

The two of us are nothing, if not one,
we are the what, the when, and the who.

You are my daughter, granddaughter, stranger:
I am your husband, and you are my wife.

from III. SELF-NECROLOGY

V

I love you because you have all of your parts
in the right place,
and you are whole, woman. Not a petal, aroma,
nor a shadow are you lacking.
Hovering in your soul,
disposed to be dew on the grass of the world,
milk of the moon in the darkened leaves.

Maybe, some day,
perhaps, you'll spot me,
perchance on an unlit lamp
in a corner of the room in which you're sleeping.
I am a stain, a dot on the wall, a scuff mark
that your eyes, despite you, go on seeing.
Maybe, like a bygone hour,
when alone you probe, inquire of
your closed, unresponsive body,
you'll recognize me.
I am a scar no longer visible,
a kiss worn away by time,
one or another love that you've put behind you.
But you are in my hands, and I'm yours,
and I am, in your arms, cinders and ash,
to dry your tears that I shed.

Where, in what place, at what unearthly hour,
will you tell me that I love you? This is urgent
because eternity is coming to an end.

Pick up my head. Put away the arm
with which I pressed your waist. Don't leave me
in the thick of your blood on that towel.

X

This sorrow has yielded tears now,
and it's good that it has.
Melibea, let's dance, make love.

Bloom of this sweet breeze that grips me,
limb of my distress:
discard me, leaf by leaf, my love.

This is your cradle, rock here in my dreams,
I'll swathe you with my blood, this is your cradle:
Let me kiss you one by one,

you women, woman, choir of surf.

Rosario, yes, Dolores when Andrea,
let me grieve you and see you.

I'm nothing but tears now;
and tear by tear, woman, I soothe you.

XI

When I was at sea, it was oceanic,
this unhurried sorrow.
Give me your mouth now:
I want to devour it with your smile.

When I was in heaven, it was sky blue,
this harrowing pain.
Give me your soul now:
I want to bite it with my teeth.

Give me nothing at all, my dear:
I'll draw you out of the wind;
drain you from the river of shadow,
the spinning light, and silence;

from the skin of things
and the blood with which I board time.
Despite your protests, you're the fountain,
and I am parched.

Don't speak to, touch or acknowledge me,
if you don't wish: I no longer exist.
I'm but the life that pursues you,
and you the death that I resist.

from IV. NIGHT FLIGHT

YOU TORMENT ME.

Gently, unendurably, you torment me.
Seize hold of my head, slit my throat.
Nothing is left of me after this love.

Among the ruins of my soul, look for me,
listen for me.
Somewhere my survivor's voice cries out,
craving your disbelief,
your enlightened silence.

Defying walls, landscapes, ages,
your face (face that appears almost real)
comes back to life, from beyond
the day on which the world first dawned.

Your face shining with such tender,
self-captivated light,
honey-traced sketch on sheets of water!

I love your eyes, I truly love them.
I am the offspring of your eyes;
like a drop from your eyes, I am.

Lift me from between your feet; gather me up
off the ground, off the shadow you walk on,
the corner of your room that in dreams you never see.
Lift me up, for I have fallen from your hands
and I want to live, live, live.

GET DOWN! A FURIOUS GALE—the machete, the wave of death—is ripping its way towards us. Get down! Hit the deck! Let them pass: the live flame with glass feet, galloping fire horses, ash hurricane, silent cold that seeps down to the rock's heart. Get down! Slip in under the warm earth, the dove that protects us beneath her moss!

Death's survivors, I say. I say daggers, cart heaped with cowheads, warehouses chock full of entrails, pots of blood, high-class restaurant managers, drunks, elegant, discreetly menstruating ladies, loners, rivers of shit girding the city, endless maze of hedges between the trees and the fog, graveyards rendered terminally ill by respectable asshole citified priests, goddamned cathedrals, buses out working the periphery, painters' markets, anthology of bilingual fucking queers...

I dream that I have my hand between your thighs, my fragile delicate bride, and that I part your lips, and place on your moist shadow the petal of a kiss. (The brush of the wing of my guardian angel wakes me, and I begin to pray in order to purify myself: in the name of the clitoris and of the foreskin, *urbi et orbi*, Amen.)

LET'S CANONIZE THE WHORES. Saturday night saints' calendar: Bety, Lola, Margot, perpetual, reconstructed virgins, temporary martyrs full of grace, wellsprings of generosity.

You give pleasure, O world-redeeming whore, and ask nothing in return but a couple of measly coins. You don't demand to be loved, respected, attended to; you don't go on like the wives with their whingeing, scolding and jealous fits. You force no one to make up or to bid you goodbye; you suck neither blood nor time; you are beyond reproach; you take the sinners to your breast, you listen to their words and dreams, you laugh and you kiss. You are patient, expert, long-suffering, wise, and free of resentment.

You deceive no one: you are honest, upright, and perfect. You name your price and you reveal yourself. You don't discriminate against the old, criminals, fools, or those of another colour. You suffer the assaults of pride, the snares of the sick; you soothe the impotent, stimulate the shy, gratify the satiated; conjure up the cure for the disenchanted. You are the drunkard's confidante, refuge of the persecuted, rest bed of he who cannot find repose.

You have educated your hands, mouth and muscles, your skin, your guts and your soul. You know how to dress and to undress; you lie down, and you move. You are precise in your rhythm, exact in your moan, docile in the ways of love.

You are freedom itself, and balance; you don't dominate or detain anyone; you don't get sentimental nor do you wait for anyone. You are pure presence, fluidity, perpetuity.

In the place in which you minister the truth and beauty of life, be it an elegant brothel, a discreet house or the makeshift beds of the poor, you are the same as a lamp or a glass of water or a slice of bread.

O whore of mine, lover, beloved, this and every day's safe haven, I recognize you, I canonize you to one side of the hypocrites and the perverts, I give you all my money, I crown you with leaves of grass and I intend to learn from you for evermore.

I LEFT MY BODY at the edge of the highway and came crying for myself. The city is huge like an enormous orphanage. Cold and comfortable, dark and lit-up like a penitentiary.

I came in search of love. I thought that love was my only refuge against the night-time bombardments. And I discovered that love could not be salvaged. Love lasts a mere instant. Corrupted by time, it does not suffer absence; it stinks with the hours, it is subject to the glands, exposed.

My little garden was full of worms. Nothing of what I left behind, I found—not a petal nor a breath of air.

What am I going to do now? I feel like, I *am*, crying. I want to gather up a few of my things—some book, a box of matches, my cigarettes, a pair of pants, a shirt maybe—and go. I don't know why or to where, but I want to go. I'm scared. I don't feel right.

What will become of my children? I hope they grow up indifferent or blissfully ignorant. We all need our distractions. That's why it's good to rock 'n' roll, do the twist, get down and mozambique.

Should we live drunk on something, as Baudelaire said we should? But this lucid drunk of time and people, isn't it a bit over the top?

I love you! I love you cockroach, María, Rosa, leprosy, Isabel, cancer, hepatitis, Gertrudis, apple, butterfly, yearling calf, wal-nut tree, river, meadow, cloud, drizzle, sun, beetle, cardboard box, I love you painted flower, feather-duster, my sweetheart! I love you. I can't live alone. I'm gone.

from **OTHER ASSORTED POEMS (1973-1993)**

THINKING IT OVER

They tell me I should exercise to lose some weight,
round your 50's when the fat and cigarettes do the damage;
they say you have to stay in good shape,
and wage the struggle against time, and old age.

Well-intentioned experts and doctor friends
push dieting regimens designed
to squeeze a few more years out of life.

I'm grateful to them all, but I have to laugh
at all such ultimately futile attempts.
(Death, too, gets a kick out of all this stuff.)

The only recommendation I take to heart
is to find a young woman for my bed,
because at this late stage
youth can only hope to reach us second hand.

YOUR NAME

In darkness, I attempt to write your name. I try to write that I love you; try to say this in the dark. I don't want anyone to come this way at three in the morning and see me pacing like a lovesick lunatic from one end of the hall to the other. Enlightened, blinded, oozing you through every pore, I utter your name with the whole of the night's silence. Tirelessly, deep in my muzzled heart, I bellow your name, repeat it again and again, and I'm certain that dawn is about to break.

THE DRUG

If you can no longer return to your left side, let yourself drift wherever you will.

It'd be good for you to forego the well's rim and venture into the underground river.

Yesterday has come and gone and who you were with it. Don't try to raise that love from its ashes: you'll only stir up eddies of dust and shadows.

Teach your heart, like a toddler, to walk again.

I told you all these things and you said:

—It's because I'm the regular fare. I swallow poison every day, and I'm hooked. What a powerful drug is love!

ACKNOWLEDGEMENTS

I wish to thank doña Josefa Rodríguez viuda de Sabines and Judith Sabines for their constant support and encouragement, and Dan Wells for producing a beautiful book. As well, the translator is deeply indebted to Stephen Henighan for his expert editorial guidance, and Verónica Garza Flores for bewitching me with the poetry of Jaime Sabines that rainy August afternoon.

* * *

"There is a way," "You torment me," "Get down! A furious gale," "Let's canonize the whores" and "I left my body" appeared in *Exile: The Literary Quarterly*

"There is a way" also appeared in *The Green Table*. Ed. Barry Callaghan

"The Lovers" appeared in *Variety Crossing 12: Transcriptions*. Ed. Dae-Tong Huh

"You have me in your hands," "Let's store this day," "You have what I'm after" and "We're here together" appeared in *Virtual Writer: Creative Writing, Literary News and Reviews* (Ireland)

ABOUT THE AUTHOR

Jaime Sabines Gutiérrez, Mexico's most influential modern poet, was born in Chiapas in 1926. His first collection, *Horal*, appeared in 1950 and met with widespread critical acclaim. Several of his later titles are considered classics, and his poetry continues to be anthologized and widely translated. He received numerous literary awards and honours over the course of his career, including the City of Mexico Prize, the National Prize for Literature, and the Belisario Domínguez Medal of Honour, the highest award bestowed by the Mexican government. Often regarded as one of the major poets of the twentieth century, he died in Mexico City in March 1999.

ABOUT THE TRANSLATOR

Colin Carberry was born in Toronto and raised in Ireland. He is the author of the poetry collections *The Crossing* (Bearing Press, 1998), *The Green Table* (Exile, 2003) and *Ceasefire in Purgatory* (Luna, 2007), and is the translator of an earlier volume of Sabines's verse. His own poetry has been translated into many languages. Colin has read from his work on radio and television, and at book fairs, embassies, literary festivals and universities in Canada, the United States, Mexico, Ireland, Bosnia-Herzegovina, and Serbia. He lives in Mexico.